# Ear[illegible]

**Written by Frank Pedersen**

**Illustrated by Graeme Tavendale**

Contents | Page



Nelson

*an International Thomson Publishing company* ITP®

# Earthquake!

**With these characters ...**

Phil Ridley

Rollo

Lucy Washington

Sergeant Jeff Finch

"This earthquake was

**Setting the scene ...**

Something is not quite right. Phil Ridley's cat, Rollo, is acting strangely and, late at night, birds are singing.

In another part of the city, at the Seismology Research Station, Lucy Washington watches the seismograph in disbelief. There's going to be an earthquake, and it's going to be a big one!

Out on the streets, Sergeant Jeff Finch watches in horror as buildings crumble and cars move about the road like toys. But what about Phil and Rollo? They are in danger and are going to need help—fast!

big—and about to get bigger!"

# Chapter 1.

Something was wrong. Phil Ridley frowned as his cat, Rollo, paced around and around the lounge room, miaowing loudly, late one evening.

"What's up, puss?" he asked, as the distressed animal pressed herself against his leg. The hairs on Rollo's back were raised. Her tail flicked furiously from side to side. She growled softly, as if she was trying to warn Phil of something.

Phil switched off the TV and looked around for Rollo's ball. Perhaps she just wants to play, he thought. He tossed the ball to Rollo, but the cat ignored it. Once again, she started to pace around the room, making strange sounds.

Phil shook his head.

"If only you could talk, Rollo," he said. "I wonder what you're trying to tell me?"

Later that evening, after Phil had put the unhappy cat in her basket, and had flopped into his own bed, another weird thing happened. Just after he turned out the lights, a blackbird perched on his bedroom window-sill and started chirping frantically.

Phil lay in bed, wondering what had disturbed the blackbird. He guessed that it must have been the neighbour's cat, prowling around outside. Obviously, Rollo had heard it too, thought Phil. No wonder she was behaving strangely! Rollo hated other cats.

But there was no cat prowling around outside. Both Rollo and the blackbird were behaving strangely for another reason.

They could hear something that Phil could not. They could hear a low, rumbling noise far off in the distance. The animals' ears were so sensitive, they could hear the vibrations of rocks, deep underground, slowly moving past each other. They were aware of a disaster about to happen. At 2.00 a.m. that morning, when most people were asleep and the streets were empty, the earthquake struck.

It started with a long, low roar that seemed to be approaching from the north of the city. Those people who were awake heard a sound like distant thunder and, as the first ripples of the earthquake sped towards the city, the ground beneath their feet started to shake. Glasses in cupboards started to tinkle. Plates started to rattle.

Within seconds, the roar grew louder, and the ground wobbled like a huge bowl of jelly. Phil Ridley woke up in alarm. What was going on? His bed was moving backwards and forwards and the chest of drawers creaked and swayed.

Still half asleep, he first thought that someone was shaking his bed. He sat up with a fright. Who was there? Then he heard the rumbling and he knew instantly—it was an earthquake! He quickly rolled over, dragging the blankets along with him, and tumbled onto the floor. Within a few seconds, he had scrambled under his bed, and lay on the shaking floor.

"Don't panic," he told himself. "It'll be over in a few seconds." Something hard bumped against his leg. He remembered the emergency kit that he kept under the bed. In the middle of the rumbling and shuddering, he had a silly thought. How long had it been since he had changed the food in his emergency kit? He wondered whether it had passed its use-by date. He hoped he wouldn't have to find out.

Even worse, he heard Rollo miaowing frantically from the laundry, where Phil imagined her cowering in her basket.

"The ground will stop shaking soon," he said, trying to reassure himself. "It's only a small earthquake, just a light tremor."

But he couldn't have been more wrong. This earthquake was big—and it was about to get bigger.

# Chapter 2.

At the same time, in another part of the city, a scientist who was working late at the Seismology Research Station leaped up from her chair. Lucy Washington rushed over to the seismograph, a machine that measured the earth's movements. There had been a few tiny earth tremors earlier that night, but they were too small for anyone to notice. That was normal in this part of the world. But what was happening now was definitely not normal!

As the seismograph shook, the line it drew told Lucy that the earthquake was one of the most severe they had ever measured. The line zoomed all over the paper.

"Oh, no!" she whispered to herself. "This really is a big one!"

In the centre of the city, some of the taller buildings were swaying gently from side to side, as the earth beneath them moved in waves. The glass in some of the older buildings cracked.

Sergeant Jeff Finch braked his police car quickly, and swerved into the middle of the empty street. He switched on his flashing lights, so no-one would accidentally drive into his police car. It was only when he switched off the engine, heard the rumble of the earthquake and felt the car sliding underneath him that he realised what was happening.

"Thank goodness it's the middle of the night," he said. He reached for his police radio, and reported the earthquake to the police station control room.

"Stay where you are, if it's safe to do so," came back the order from his commander, Police Chief Southfield. "Remain inside your car."

By 2.03 a.m., the rumbling grew quieter, and the ground stopped its weird, wavy movement.

Beneath his bed, Phil listened carefully for the slightest sound. He wasn't going anywhere until he was sure it was safe. Rollo had stopped miaowing. He hoped she was OK. He knew the poor cat would be terrified.

When the rumbling stopped, Sergeant Finch opened his car door and looked around at the buildings on both sides of the street. Fortunately, none of the windows had burst outwards into the street, but many of them were cracked. He'd have to try and contact the building owners to warn them about their broken windows. You never know who might take advantage of a broken shop window at this time of the night, he thought grimly.

Lucy Washington watched with a feeling of relief as the seismograph line slowly returned to normal. She looked back at the huge wavy lines that marked the earthquake of a few minutes ago. She checked the numbers on the side of the graph paper.

"Five on the Richter Scale," she noted. "That's severe."

Then, just as she thought about the report she would write about the earthquake, her eyes widened. She stared at the seismograph. This couldn't be happening!

The pen on the seismograph was shaking again.

# Chapter 3.

It was now 2.04 a.m. The lines were becoming larger and larger every second. Another earthquake was on its way. And from the lines swinging wildly from one edge of the paper to the other, Lucy knew that this earthquake would be a lot larger than the last one.

Even Lucy, who had seen the seismograph record a hundred earthquakes, had an awful feeling in her stomach. She dived under her desk. She was going to need all the solid protection she could get. With an enormous, shuddering lurch, the giant earthquake hit the city.

In the centre of the city, Sergeant Finch leapt towards his car, narrowly avoiding a shower of glass, as dozens of windows burst from their frames, high above him. He furiously twisted the ignition key and reversed at high speed. One of the older brick buildings twisted dangerously, and bricks fell onto the street. Then, Sergeant Finch watched in horror as the building slowly disintegrated and collapsed.

A huge cloud of dust rose in the air, and his whole car was pelted with fragments of brick and glass.

Sergeant Finch was shaking. He stopped his car in an open space, away from the buildings, and stared at the devastation that the earthquake had caused.

Lucy Washington crouched in terror underneath her desk as filing cabinets bounced across the floor and emptied their contents all around her. Fortunately, the people at the seismic centre had known that earthquakes could be strong enough to topple over heavy bookcases, so most things were screwed into the walls. But all their contents, including books, papers and magazines, were flung off the shelves.

The lights swung crazily from the ceiling. There was a huge crash as some of the plaster from the ceiling fell on top of her desk.

Lucy huddled close to the back of her desk and closed her eyes. Even though she had been studying earthquakes for years, she never imagined she'd be caught in the middle of a really destructive, powerful quake. She felt helpless and tiny in the middle of such awesome, out-of-control power!

Wrapped up in his blankets, Phil Ridley felt his chest of drawers topple over on top of his bed. There was a mighty thud as it hit the mattress.

Now he was really scared. He heard a loud, creaking sound and then a deafening tearing noise. His house was twisting and turning on its foundations. Suddenly, the front part of his roof collapsed. The beams holding the roof up had been shaken loose from the walls. Tonnes of wood and plaster and metal crashed down. Phil Ridley was trapped! His only hope was that the emergency services people would find him quickly!

As the earthquake died down, Lucy Washington opened her eyes and looked at the wreckage at the seismology research station.

It had been designed by earthquake engineers to withstand the strongest earthquake, so the walls and the roof still stood. But inside, there was chaos. Files and paper and books lay scattered all around. Chairs lay toppled on their sides. Even though the ground had stopped shaking, the lights strung from the ceiling were still swaying from side to side. In the middle of the disaster, Lucy heard an absurdly ordinary sound. The phone was ringing.

# Chapter 4.

"This is Police Chief Southfield," said a voice urgently. "I need to know if we can expect any more earthquakes."

"It's impossible to predict," replied Lucy. She crawled over to the seismograph and read the graph paper with a look of amazement.

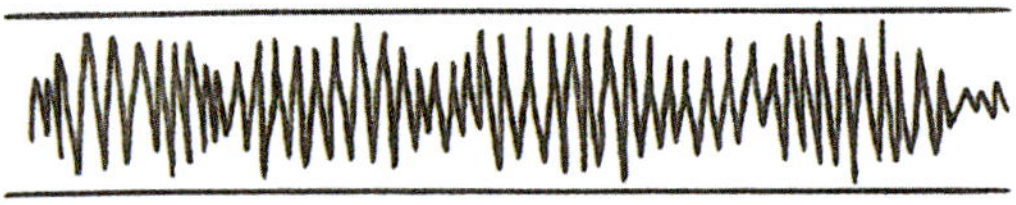

"That last one was a six on the Richter Scale," she told the police chief. "Ten times larger than the first one. There's only a slim chance of another earthquake bigger than that, so soon afterwards."

"That's a relief," said the police chief. "Thanks."

"But, Chief," warned Lucy quickly. "Remember, it's normal for a lot of smaller earthquakes to happen as the earth settles down again. Tell people to take care in damaged buildings. Even a small aftershock can cause walls or roofs to collapse."

"Thanks for the reminder," said the police chief. He hung up.

Lucy looked at her watch. It was ten minutes past two. It wouldn't be long before the centre was crowded with scientists and other people who worked at the research centre, all wanting to know how severe the earthquakes were. And there was other work to be done. She had to contact the other seismic research centres around the country to find out when the earthquake had been recorded by their machines.

By calculating how long it had taken for the earthquake to travel around the country, the scientists could work out where the earthquake's hypocentre had been.

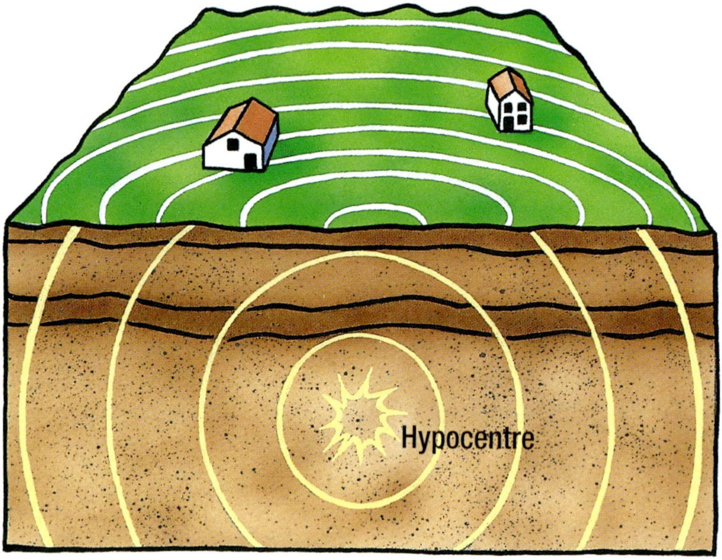


That was where the earthquake had started. That was the place where the rocks deep beneath the earth's surface had been pushed past each other with a huge force. This movement had unleashed the waves of energy that, in a few short minutes, had brought disaster to her city.

By the time the sun rose the next morning, Sergeant Finch was exhausted. He had spent the night, along with every other available policeman and policewoman, helping the emergency services check houses and buildings for people. The night air had been filled with eerie flashing blue and red lights, and the sounds of sirens.

But the sight of the city in the morning light shocked Sergeant Finch even more. All around were piles of rubble and stones and bricks. Smashed glass lay in the streets. Cars that had been parked neatly the night before were tossed onto front lawns or into the middle of the road, where they lay at crazy angles.

Most people had been home asleep when the earthquake struck, which was lucky, thought Sergeant Finch. He shuddered to think what might have happened if the disaster had happened in the afternoon, when the city's streets and buildings were full of office workers, shoppers and children.

Sergeant Finch was working with an ambulance team and an emergency services team. They were checking for injured people, house by house, street by street. Fortunately, most people had known what to do, and had sheltered under beds, desks, or doorways. Most of the injuries were minor.

As they turned a corner and travelled down another street, they saw a house that was very badly damaged. The whole front of the roof had collapsed. Another group of emergency workers were trying to clear the wreckage. When they saw Sergeant Finch's group, they called out for help.

"We've got someone under all this," yelled one of the emergency workers. "Come and give us a hand!"

# Chapter 5.

Jeff and his team started pulling at the bricks, timber and pieces of sheet metal. Within a few minutes, they could see an outline of a bed, under a pile of clothes, plaster, and furniture.

Jeff crawled through the rubble until he reached the bed. He shone his torch under it and was greeted with a sight that almost made him laugh. A man, covered in dust, was calmly lying on his elbows under the bed, eating a chocolate biscuit. A can of lemonade stood beside him.

"Sorry to disturb your breakfast, sir. Are you okay?" asked Sergeant Finch, wriggling closer to the bed.

"I've had better mornings," replied the man, smiling weakly at Sergeant Finch. "I could do with a cup of tea."

Sergeant Finch reached out to grab the man's hand. Slowly, he eased him out from under the bed that had saved his life. Together, they crawled backwards out of the rubble.

An enormous cheer came from the emergency workers who gathered around.

From between the workers' legs, a cat wound its way up to the man. The cat purred and rubbed against his leg. The man lent down, picked up the cat, and gave it a big hug.

"I'm afraid Rollo will have to make do with chocolate biscuits for breakfast this morning," grinned the man. "I didn't think to keep any *cat* food in my emergency kit."

"I'm sure she is glad just to see you," replied Sergeant Finch, smiling.

"Yes, and I'm glad to see her—and the daylight—again!" replied Phil.

Sergeant Jeff Finch nodded.

"We'll make it," Phil told himself, as he looked down the street at the ruined houses.

"Okay, people, let's go!  The next house is waiting!" ordered Sergeant Finch wearily.

*The earthquakes had caused an enormous amount of damage to the city, and wrecked people's homes. It would take many months of hard work and effort to rebuild people's homes and buildings. But two things that the earthquakes hadn't been able to destroy were people's spirit and determination.*

*Those things, more than anything else, would be needed in the coming months.*

# "Earthquake!"

Like an angry animal, the earthquake roars,
Like a stormy wave, the earthquake crashes,
With a vicious shake, the earthquake destroys,
With a threatening silence, the earthquake waits,
Humans, powerless, scatter like ants in the rain.